Growing Su(

A Beginner's Guide to Succulent Gardening

Harry Choi

Copyright © 2020 **Harry Choi**

All rights reserved.

ISBN: 9798664314687

DEDICATION

The author and publisher have provided this e-book to you for your personal use only. You may not make this e-book publicly available in any way. Copyright infringement is against the law. If you believe the copy of this e-book you are reading infringes on the author's copyright, please notify the publisher at: https://us.macmillan.com/piracy

Contents

Tips for Succulent Beginners 1

Mistakes when Growing 10

Best Succulents for Beginners 19

Projects 32

Tips for Succulent Beginners

CHOOSING THE RIGHT SUCCULENTS

It is common thing to worry that as newbie to gardening, you might end up killing all your plants. Even low-maintenance plants like succulents can get tricky sometimes so choosing a beginner plant is very important.

Most succulent prefer full sun, outdoor to thrive. Nevertheless, if you fancy an indoor plant, there are varieties of succulent that can tolerate shade and grow indoor. For example, succulents of Haworthia genres generally prefer filtered light rather than direct sunlight. Other succulents, like Senecio String of Pearls or Donkey Tail also perform well given some shade.

Remember, even if you grow them indoor, you should put them in a window sill where they can receive at least 4-6 hours of sunlight.

If you plant to grow succulents outside and want plants that are resilient enough, either Sempervivum or Cactus would be a great choice.

Sempervivum are among the most cold-hardy plants that can withstand temperature as low as -30F. Plus, they show great color variation after being cold-stressed. Meanwhile, though not as hardy as Sempervivum, Cactus are infamous for being a super low-maintenance plant.

Growing Succulents

WATER

Watering right is extremely important to succulent.

Why? Succulents are different from normal plants. Their natural habitat are mostly in dessert, which means they have develop the ability to store water in leaves and have high heat-tolerance.

So, succulent do not need as much water as normal plant. However, it is important to know WHEN and HOW to water them.

WHEN: only water your succulent when the soil is completely dry up. To check, you can use a moisture meter or simple use a chopstick and stick it up the drainage hole. If the dirt on the chopstick feel moist, it it not yet time to water again. Depending on the weather and temperature, it could be once every week or once every 10-14 days.

HOW: DO NOT water on the leaves of the succulent, only water on the soil. If you live in dry and sunny areas, it might be fine. However, in humid conditions, it would lead to rotten leaves. Also, remember to give your succulent a real good soak every time you water them. A tip to know if the amount of water is right is seeing if there is water dripping out of the drainage hole.

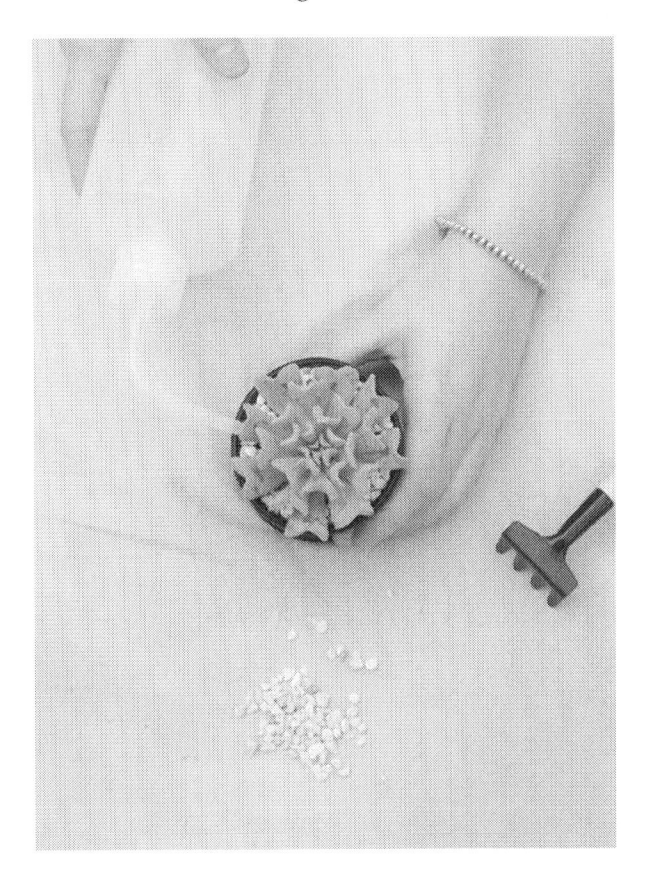

CHOOSE A BREATHABLE POT WITH DRAINAGE HOLE

There are different varieties of pot you can use to grow your succulent. However, they should be breathable and have good drainage hole. Succulent do not like to sit in wet for a long time since it makes their roots to absorb too much water and quickly rot.

If you are new to growing succulent, make sure you use pot with drainage hole. Terrarium or pot without drainage is a big no-no. Terra cotta pot is often recommended for beginners. Made of porous clay, terra cotta keeps soils cool and dry out quite fast, especially in sunny location.

USING SOIL MIX FOR SUCCULENT AND CACTUS

We could not stress this enough: DO NOT use normal soil mix for your succulent. Normal soil are great to retain water and mineral but succulents need well-drained soil. If the soil hold too much water, your succulents can easily get root rot.

LIGHT AND TEMPERATURE

Succulent generally need at least 4-6 hours of morning sunlight. Some succulents have high heat-tolerant but many don't like scorching sun. Sunburned or browning is a common sign when your succulents are getting too much sunlight. When it gets too sunny, it is better to move them to a place like south east window sill where they get a healthy amount of filtered sunlight.

Although succulents can tolerate shade, they don't like to stay in place lack of sunlight either. If you happen to find your succulent stretching out or the gap between the leaves are widening, it is a sign that they need more sunlight. You might consider using grow light to provide enough sunlight for your succulent to stay compact.

The ideal temperature for succulents are from 60 to 80°F. If you live in colder zone, remember to bring your succulent inside when temperature fall below 40 F.

GROOM YOUR PLANTS

Insects and pests like to habor over dead or decaying foliage so keep your plants clean and tidy is a good way to keep them healthy and happy. Get rid of dry or rotten leaves often and check your plant roots when there is sign of overwater.

Mistakes when Growing

Placing Succulents in Poorly Lit Spaces

Okay, so you heard that succulents are versatile and have been adapted to growing in harsh conditions. Since they grow in deserts and literally anywhere, they can even survive in closets or in the basement. Wrong.

Every green plant, regardless of its adaptations requires sun light to survive (remember photosynthesis?). True, there are some low sun light succulents that can do well in little light, but they also need to be exposed to sun light for a minimum number of hours every day.

What's more, minimalist home designs are increasingly becoming popular by the day with succulents as the go-to indoor plants to achieve the style. These elegant and simple plants make a perfect fit for such designs.

However, most home decorating designs don't make provisions for stuffing many plants on the windowsill, minimalist especially.

But with succulents, light is critical and tucking that Sedeveria at your living room's corner is just begging it to die or become etiolated. You don't want your succulents looking stretched, pale and lanky.

Majority of succulents require a minimum of four to eight hours of sunlight every day. This helps them to make food through photosynthesis so that they can be healthy. If growing succulents indoors, it's recommended to place them on a south or west facing window. During summer, you can take them outside and let them bask in the sun during morning or late afternoon hours. If the natural lighting in your home is needing, a grow lamp may get the job done.

Failure to Observe Fertilizing Best Practices

A number of succulent gardeners believe that succulents don't need fertilizer. While most succulents can do perfectly well without any fertilizer, it's important to note that nutrients are necessary for any plant. Feeding your plants may increase their growth rate and give them a healthier look.

A common mistake that's prevalent among beginners in feeding succulents is overfeeding. It's recommended to feed your plants three to four times a year. The best time for this is during summer or spring when your plants are actively growing. Succulents are generally dormant during winter so avoid feeding them during this time.

Crowding too many Succulents in One Space

Growing different succulents in one place presents a spectacular aesthetic. And to some extent, succulents can get along with this better than other plants. However, squeezing many of them in a single space presents a few problems. Competition for nutrients becomes fierce which may lead to malnourishment.

Additionally, excessive crowding of succulents may encourage pest infestations and even the spread of mold. Such a combination of succulent killers is deadly and may wipe out your entire collection.

Not Giving Your Succulents Enough Water

Another succulent faux-pax is the notion that they can survive without any water. Though xerophytic and adapted to desert conditions, succulents require enough water in order to store some in their leaves.

A desert may experience long spells of drought but when it rains, it pours. It's recommended to mimic such watering as succulents are adapted to this.

Let loose a deluge on your succulents and wait till the soil is bone dry to water again. Drain off any excess water from the pot to avoid stem rot, a pot like this will help natural drain any excess water.

Planting Succulents with Non-Succulents

Different plant arrangements are just gorgeous. No doubt succulents look good when paired with some ferns or moss varieties.

Unfortunately, that can only be done temporarily.

Succulents have very different growing conditions as compared with other home plants. Basil needs water like every six hours or else it'll begin to wilt. Similarly, a moss plant will thrive in an environment that's moist throughout.

On the other side of the ring, succulents can't stand being wet. It's literally impossible to have a cohesion without one of the plants dying.

This is also true for some succulent groups. While a few succulents can go on without water for weeks, some need to be watered on a weekly basis.

Using Inappropriate Planters or Pots

Succulents appear even more beautiful when planted in fashionable planters. However, if your container is jeopardizing the growth of your plants, you'll soon end up with an empty planter.

Succulents are prone to root rot. This happens when they sit in wet soil for too long. Soil in containers without a drainage hole takes much longer to dry out increasing the chances of root rot.

Similarly, partially-closed containers leads to higher levels of humidity around your succulents. This is risky as it also promotes rot especially in the leaves and stem.

You can never go wrong with Terra cotta, wood or hypertufa containers.

Misting Succulents

This emanates from the belief that succulents don't need a lot of water and so misting is the way to go. Nothing could be further from the truth…

Not only is misting a terrible way to water succulents, it also promotes leaf rot as most people who mist succulents do it on a daily basis. Leaves rotting is due to the fact that most of the water remains in the leaves for extended periods of time. This is dangerous for succulents such as Kalanchoe tomentosa.

Using Standard Potting Soil When Planting Succulents

Succulents may be pretty, but they're a little picky when it comes to soil requirements. Standard potting soil may work for other house plants but not succulents. These plants are adapted to well-draining, grainy desert soils.

Regular potting soil retains water making the soil wet for a long time – succulents' greatest nightmare. The potting soil being wet for extended periods doesn't just go well with succulents. They're susceptible to root rot, something you wouldn't want to deal with as a beginner.

When it comes to which soil to choose, our best bet is a commercial cacti mix. This is available online and you don't even have to break the bank.

In case you're feeling a bit creative and you wouldn't mind getting your hands dirty, you can custom make your own cacti mix. Simply mix equal portions of garden soil with perlite, pumice or building sand. Avoid using soil with peat moss as it promotes water retention.

Over Watering Succulents

Loving succulents is okay. However, love them with moderation as they'll easily perish when showered with excess love. Most house plant lovers like their plants looking vibrant and healthy. They try to achieve this by watering their plants every waking minute. Not so with succulents. Remember root rot – it's real.

When it comes to watering succulents, the rule of thumb is to allow the soil to dry out completely in between watering. Drench your plants and let the excess water to drain out. Minimize feeding your succulents with water during winter. For most succulents, avoid watering the leaves and only water from below. The reason for this is that one, leaves don't take in water and something else, you're making them susceptible to rot.

Keeping Plants Root Bound for too Long

Most succulents fit perfectly well in small planters. You can even use our hidden cactus mug as a planter for the smaller succulent plants.

Nevertheless, plant roots require enough room for growth. If roots overgrow their pot and stay in that condition, desiccation problems will ensue because water won't be absorbed properly. Additionally, uptake of nutrients and minerals may be a problem leading to a weak plant.

Succulents are slow growers and determining when to repot may prove to be daunting. The best tip we can think of is repotting as soon as roots start peeping through the drainage hole.

Best Succulents for Beginners

1. Kalanchoe

Kalanchoe can go for weeks without water, and this trait makes them very easy to maintain! They overgrow quickly for a succulent and produce beautiful flowers of different colors. Blossfeldiana variety produces some of the longest blooming flowers in the plant world!

Easy to grow Varieties:

- Kalanchoe blossfeldiana

- Kalanchoe pinnata
- Kalanchoe beharensis
- Kalanchoe popphyrocalyx and manginii

2. Agave

Agave plants are popular as succulents with large leaves and pointed tips. These plants can survive well in full sun to partial shade. Also, they are drought tolerant, and when it comes to soil preference, they do well in any well-draining soil.

Easy to grow Varieties:

- Agave attenuata
- Agave parviflora
- Agave Tequilana Azul
- Agave victoria-reginae

Fun Fact: Tequila is distilled from the fermented juice of the Central American century plant Agave tequilana.

3. Echeveria

Native to Central America, Echeveria is well suited for outdoor habitat. They require low watering, fewer nutrients, and will even thrive on an extended period of neglect. Echeveria is a slow-growing succulent and reaches a height and width of 12 inches, at its best.

Easy to grow Varieties:

- Black Prince Echeveria
- Echeveria elegans
- Echeveria colorata
- Princess Blue Echeveria

4. Aloe

Although Aloe is undemanding, you do have to keep a few things in mind. Water the plant only after the soil turns dry and keep them in a bright spot. It is also known as the wonder plant, thanks to its gel that has been used for its many therapeutic properties for thousands of years.

Easy to grow Varieties:

- Aloe Vera

- Climbing Aloe
- Flow Aloe
- Lace Aloe
- Aloe juvenna
- Aloe 'White lightning.'

5. Crassula

There are many varieties of crassula, and all of them are easy to grow. The most popular amongst them is the jade plant, also known as money tree or lucky tree. Propagate them from offsets, division, or leaf cuttings. Like other succulents, they also do not need watering too often. In summers, they go dormant and need scarcer watering.

Easy to grow Varieties:

- Jade Plant
- Crassula muscosa
- Crassula perforata (Necklace Plant)
- Moon Glow Crassula
- Crassula rupestris

6. Haworthia

Haworthia is commonly known as the zebra plant because of the stripes present on the leaves. Some genus of this succulent has transparent foliage and makes a beautiful addition for home decor. They are hardier than other succulents and can survive in low light.

Avoid overwatering for optimum growth.

Easy to grow Varieties:

- Haworthia transiens
- Haworthia truncata
- Haworthia chocolate

7. Snake Plant

According to research conducted by NASA, this plant purifies the indoor air by absorbing nitrogen oxides, formaldehyde, and other toxins. Consider them as the most tolerant plant; the snake plant will remain healthy for weeks without care. It is the best choice for a houseplant as they stay fresh, even in dim lighting.

Easy to grow Varieties:

- Sansevieria trifasciata 'Mother-in law's Tongue.'
- Sansevieria trifasciata 'Twist.'
- Sansevieria trifasciata 'Golden hahnii'

8. Faucaria

One of the best succulents for beginners, it is also known as "tiger jaws" because the edges of the leaves look spiny and form a jaw-like, ferocious shape. It grows colorful flowers in shades of yellow, white to pink, which start to bloom at the beginning of winter or in fall.

They can survive extreme heat but need good drainage.

Easy to grow Varieties:

- Faucaria boscheana
- Faucaria felina
- Faucaria tigerina
- Faucaria gratiae

9. Gasteria

This plant also goes with the name Ox Tongue, Cow Tongue, or Lawyer's Tongue because its leaves resemble the shape of a tongue. Its flowers look like the stomach, and therefore it is also named Gasteria (Gaster is Latin for the stomach). Just like other succulents, it thrives in fast-draining soil and bright, indirect sunlight.

Easy to grow Varieties:

- Gasteria verrucosa
- Gasteria maculata
- Gasteria glomerata

10. Sedum

Also commonly known as lamb's tail, burro's tail, or horse's tail, they are excellent as hanging plants or trailers. This plant will grow without much attention. When grown in the full sun, the plants turn into a visual delight because of the orange-red highlights!

Easy to grow Varieties:

- Sedum 'Autumn Joy'
- Sedum spectabile 'Brilliant.'
- Sedum 'Vera Jamison'

- Sedum 'Black Jack'

11. Sempervivum

Sempervivum is a task-free and 'no fuss' plant that thrives on neglect. Plant them in rock gardens, container gardens, rooftop gardens, and rock walls; those attractive foliage go well with all. You can also propagate its offsets, anywhere you like, easily.

Easy to grow Varieties:

- Sempervivum arachnoideum 'Cobweb houseleek'
- Sempervivum ' Engle'
- Sempervivum marmoreum 'Brunneifolium'
- Sempervivum 'Pippin'

12. Adromischus

Native to Southern Africa, it forms bright green tubular, wide, and short recurved lobes. The plant resembles baby's feet, the undulated small 'toes' and hairy stems are two properties of this easy-to-grow succulent. The hairy texture helps in holding moisture and prevents the plant from drying. Just be careful not to overwater the plant.

Easy to grow Varieties:

- Adromischus cristatus 'Crinkle leaf plant'
- Adromischus cooperi
- Adromischus maculatus

Projects

Succulents are a creative gardener's dream! They come in all sorts of shapes, sizes, and colors, and they thrive so well planted in so many different containers that you can come up with a million unique ways to grow and display these sweet little plants. Whether you want to grow them outdoors or in (or hang them on the door as a living wreath!), in tiny planters or large ones, these plants are the perfect way to find and show your unique gardening style. Some of the succulent projects in this list use living succulent plants in artistic ways, while some of them draw on succulents as inspiration to create art made from different materials.

Set a Place in the Garden for a Succulent Chair Planter

This lush succulent planter is a fun and funky way to repurpose an old chair that doesn't have a seat. If people can't sit in it anymore, succulents can! Choose a wide variety of succulents in different colors, sizes, and shapes, planting the tallest ones at the back for the most pleasing design.

Wooden Letters

Add succulents to wooden letters for some fresh decor. Cover the whole letter or just choose part of it for a focal point.

A Sweet and Succulent Valentine

This heart-shaped succulent planter is a sweet gift at any time of year! It's planted in a tin leftover from Valentine's chocolates. Not many plants would grow in such a shallow container, but succulents thrive and look gorgeous.

A sweet and sugar-free way to say I love you - make a succulent valentine

These adorable snow globes are made using recycled jars and artificial succulents. They have all the whimsy and nostalgia of a traditional snow globe, but with a modern, garden-themed twist!

Lion's Head Planter

I love how my succulents look atop this lion's head planter! Succulents are gorgeous but simple enough to compliment an ornate planter like this one without making it look too busy.

Find Peace of Mind in a Mini Succulent Zen Garden

Small Zen gardens made with sand are used for practicing meditation by creating designs in the sand mindfully. We love that idea and wanted to create my own version with a little greenery. The Garden Therapy solution? Succulents!

Salad Bowl Planter

For a sleek, minimalist display, plant succulents directly into a bowl. As they grow, the succulents will start to trail over the edges and down the sides a bit, making it look even better.

Shooting Star Succulent Planter

Many succulents look like a starburst, with their pointy leaves and rosette shapes. This upcycled star-shaped planter looks beautiful planted with a galaxy of succulents in different colors.

Beeswax Succulent Mason Jar Candles

We love succulents and we love making candles, so obviously we have a succulent candle project! You won't believe how easy these are to make. They make a great gift that will bring an instant smile to any fellow succulent-lover's face.

Birdcage Succulent Planter

Pretty vintage birdcages seem to be everywhere these days. They make a lovely hanging planter. Grow succulents inside and watch them trail down elegantly. Hang just one of these in the backyard for a beautiful focal point, or make a bunch and hang them around to decorate a special outdoor event like a summer wedding.

Make a Living Semper-Viva Succulent Wreath

This gorgeous wreath is one of our favorite succulent projects because it is just so lush and vibrant. Living wreaths are wonderful because they are like a mini garden on your door and they don't fade quickly like fresh wreaths can. Succulents will root and grow right in a wreath form and they will spread and fill in as the plants get more established.

Succulent Grapevine Wreath

You can also make a succulent wreath using a grapevine base, you will just need to refresh the plants every now and then to keep it looking its best!

Succulent Frame

If you want something more unique than a framed painting, how about framing some living plants? You can see how I made this picture perfect succulent artwork in my book Garden Made.

Stunning Terracotta Pot Succulent Centerpiece

A collection of extra flowerpots, a simple white pillar candle, and assorted succulents come together to make this rustic and unique centerpiece. Set it up on an outdoor table and wow everyone who visits your patio this summer.